Published by Evans Brothers Limited
2A Portman Mansions
Chiltern Street
London W1U 6NR

© Evans Brothers Limited 2006

First published 2006

Printed in China by WKT Co., Ltd

British Library Cataloguing in Publication data.

Powell, Jillian
Thomas has Autism. - (Like Me, Like You)
1. Autism - Juvenile literature 2. Autism - Juvenile
literature
I. Title
362.1'989285882

ISBN 0 237 53033 3 42619535 2/10
13-digit ISBN (from 1 January 2007) 978 0 237 53033 4

Acknowledgements

The author and publisher would like to thank the following
for their help with this book:

Thomas Wildsmith and the Wildsmith family, the staff and
pupils of Claytons Combined School, and everyone at the
Rainbow Club.

The publisher would also like to thank the National Autistic
Society for their help in the preparation of this book.

All photographs by Gareth Boden

Credits

Editor: Julia Bird
Designer: Mark Holt
Production: Jenny Mulvanny

The National
Autistic Society

LIKE ME LIKE YOU

Thomas has AUTISM

JILLIAN POWELL

Evans

Hi, my name is Thomas and I have autism. My brain works differently from most people's, which means I find it hard to communicate. I also have some **learning difficulties**.

I live at home with my mum and dad, my brother Christopher and our pet fish. I like playing tennis, riding my bike and singing and dancing to music. I also like playing ball with Christopher.

AUTISM

About 1 in every 110 people has autism. Boys are four times more likely to develop autism than girls.

At breakfast, Mum gives me some fish oils. Some doctors say that they may help my brain to think and learn. Mum makes sure I have a healthy diet, too.

MANAGING AUTISM

A special diet or vitamins may be used to help manage autism, on a doctor's advice.

After breakfast, I look at some of my comics. I can't read very well yet, but I like looking at the pictures and enjoy the bright colours.

Having autism means I sometimes behave a bit differently from most people. I like keeping things tidy. When I have finished playing, I like to put all my toys away in the right order.

I like to check everywhere to see if things are dusty, even in other people's houses! Also if I see a door or drawer open, I like to shut it so everything looks tidy.

I go to a **special unit** for children with autism at my school. I have most of my lessons in the unit, but I join a class in the main school for subjects like music, P.E. and swimming.

Every day, I look at pictures on my board to find out what I'm going to do. I like having a plan for my day. I get upset if I don't know what will happen next, and I feel happier when I have a routine to follow.

13

As well as autism, I also have some learning difficulties.

I'm just learning to read and write and to add up numbers.

My teacher shows me **flashcards** which help me to

remember words.

I practise writing my name and copying letters and numbers. My teacher helps me to write by pressing on my hand when I hold my pen.

AUTISTIC SPECTRUM

Every child with autism is different. Some have learning difficulties, others do not. All find other people hard to understand and the world may seem confusing to them. A very few have a special talent, in music, art or maths, for example.

Today I'm doing a puzzle from my work tray. I have not done this puzzle before, so my teacher showed me what to do. Now I'm having a go on my own.

When I have finished all my work, I get a book or a toy to play with. I often choose a book and take it to the reading corner. I like sitting quietly on my own after I have been working hard.

Sometimes we play
games to help us
with our speech.
Today we're singing
"What's in the
box?" We have to
take things out
of the box and say
what they are.
I have taken rain
out of the box!

I go to a room called the sensory room to have special lessons. The sensory room has different lights and sounds which stimulate my senses. I'm playing with lights today.

Once a week, I go to Rainbow, which is a club for children who have autism. On the way, Mum makes sure I look out for cars and don't run out into the road. She also helps me cross the road safely at the zebra crossing.

When we get to the club, I have to find my name on a list at the door and stick it onto the board as I go in.

At Rainbow club, we can draw or make crafts, and play board games together. Today I'm playing a game with my friend Beth. I like getting all the pieces in the right place.

MAKING FRIENDS

People with autism often find it hard to make friends, as they have trouble understanding other people.

Today, we're playing with a balloon. I have to try to keep it up in the air as long as I can. I always have lots of energy to run around and play.

Then we sit in a circle for music time. The music team sings a song and we play along. I like playing the **tambourine** and the drums. I love listening to the beat.

After music, we have a break to have a drink. Sometimes we can play with the bubble machine. It's great fun!

ASPERGER SYNDROME

Some people have a form of autism called Asperger syndrome. They may find it hard to communicate with others, but do not usually have learning difficulties.

25

Having autism means I sometimes find it more difficult to do things than other children. When I ride my bike, I need to wear weights on my legs. This helps me to push down on the pedals.

But I can still enjoy all my favourite things like music, comics and tennis, and I love bouncing on the trampoline!

Glossary

Asperger syndrome a form of autism

Flashcards cards that show words or numbers that are used in teaching

Learning difficulties when someone needs extra help with reading and writing and other skills

Special unit part of a school where classes are held for pupils with special needs

Tambourine a musical instrument played by shaking or striking it

Index

Further Information

UNITED KINGDOM
The National Autistic Society
Helpline: 0845 070 4004
www.autism.org.uk
Lots of information, advice and support for
families with autism

UNITED STATES OF AMERICA
Autism Society of America
Tel: 301 657 0881
www.autism-society.org
Includes links to related organisations
and charities.

AUSTRALIA
Autism Australia
Tel: 617 3889 8572
www.autismaustralia.com.au
Website of a support group for families with
autism, including personal stories, poems,
information and links.

NEW ZEALAND
Autistic Association of New Zealand
Tel: (03) 332 1038
www.autismnz.org.nz
Information and news for people with autism or
Asperger syndrome and their families and carers.

BOOKS
Everybody is Different
Fiona Bleach, The National Autistic Society,
2001

I have Autism – What's That?
Kate Doherty et al, Down Lisburn Trust, 2004

My Special Brother Rory
Ellie Fairfoot, The National Autistic Society,
2004

What Does it Mean to have Autism?
Louise Spilsbury, Heinemann Library 2002

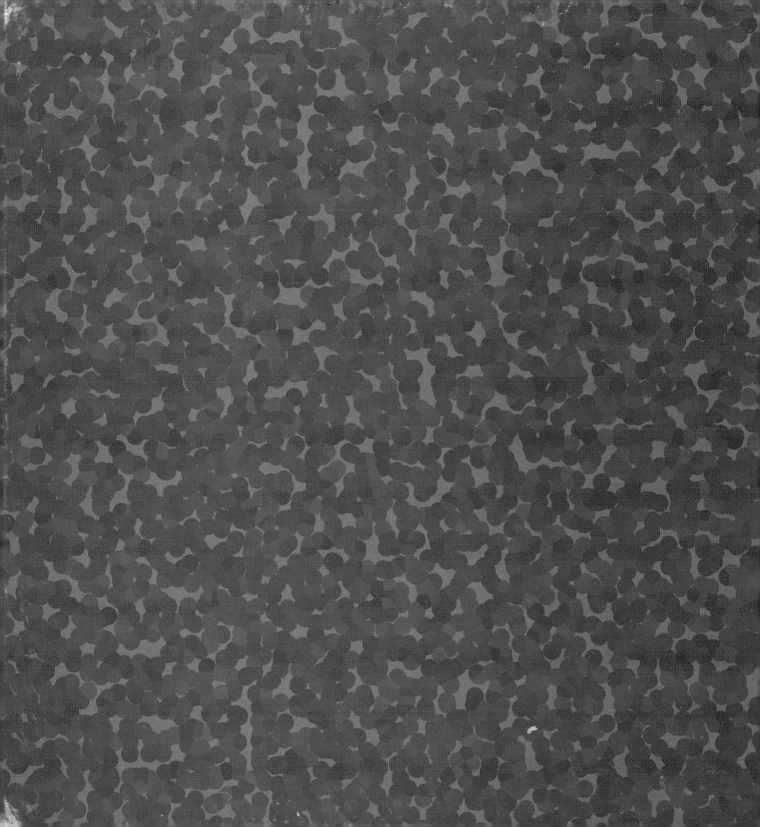